# A cataclysmic lack of Harmony

Nebulus

 pencil

ISBN 978-93-5610-019-0
© Nebulus 2021
Published in India 2021 by Pencil

*A brand of*
One Point Six Technologies Pvt. Ltd.
123, Building J2, Shram Seva Premises,
Wadala Truck Terminal, Wadala (E)
Mumbai 400037, Maharashtra, INDIA
**E** connect@thepencilapp.com
**W** www.thepencilapp.com

# Author biography

An extravagant, eccentric,

chaotic person, made of

interrelated facets and

intricate geometries of

brambles. Enthusiastic by

nature but easily prone to

boredom, with an indisputable

exuberance, a dose of

competitiveness, a burning

passion and a portion of

determination per day, I paint

my days, draw the stairs that

lead to a transitory state of

bliss and oblivion, project

that incandescence inside my

heart, write the melody of an

out of tune existence, search

for the inner secrets of space

and time, and compose the

notes of a mellifluous, quiet

solitude. Admire me, while I'm

fluctuating through my own

ethereal design, in a

labyrinth of thorns over the

effervescent skyline, trying

to absorb what the vivid

universe has to offer to its

own creatures.

# CONTENTS

# Rain

Tip

    Tap

   Tip

  Tap

   Tip

    Tap

   Tip

Here on this bed I lie,

    sleepless.

Around me the

      darkness,

No light can be seen.

Like a sailor

Fighting storms and seas,

Constantly in danger:

Overwhelming

       waves   ~ ~

Crashing against my colourless

   s

  k

   i

  n

Deteriorate whatever you find in your path,

Nothing must be left how it was:

Wash away the tiniest of the

i     p     r     e     t     o     s

   m     e     f     c     I     n

Turn the present around,

Remind me of the destructive

past ←

And hang false expectations

To that blank wall:   → the future.

      up

Throw me ↑, push me ↓

down,

Crack my bones, hunt my heart:

Your eager hands wrapped

around          lifeless mouth.

my

Tip

Tap

Tip

Tap

Tip

Tap

Tip

...Silence.

Alone,

You left me,

Waging an eternal and impossible war

Through the flames of your disinterest,

breathless.

Talking to me, as if I was there,

why are you wasting your          breath?

We used to talk for days and days,

Filling the room with warm timeless

L a u g h t e r

Monologuing under the moonlight,

hiding among those bright stars,

as if we


owned


the night,

riding the coaster of our youth,

RECKLESS and uNbUrDeNeD.

Now, nothing left but silent monosyllables,

f a d i ng into the (cold) darkness

of our empty memories.

A

blurred vision

taking over

the view of you and I,

now only the

memory

of  y

    o

       u    and I.

# Malaise

Vitriolic was the feeling in her heart,

"Pervicacious" her middle name.

Her judgment obfuscated

by an obiquitous fog

Soul and mind - just a dichotomy

A perfunctory action is nothing

Compared to an eternal dissatisfaction

She's just an anomaly of the world,

Made of her life a frivolous theatre

Not capitulating to their requests,

She found herself drowning

The abyss is deep,

Deeper than she could ever imagine

No breathing creature out there,

Holding Hope's fragile ropes,

Would be able to hear the inaudible utterance

Solitude and acedia scratching her heart,

Phosphenes is what she sees

Left fragmented she stares at her life,

Spending each day in solitude

The clock sentences her to a greater escape,

Navigating through space and time

Towards an inevitable ultimate destination:

Death.

## Lustrous Panacea

Equanimity is what I need:

I'm not gregarious, that's axiomatic,

Living in an uncertain world, the Earth,

Feeling flummoxed is not improbable.

Paradoxically flabbergasted and blasé,

A nefarious faith precociously opens its doors,

While a mellifluous euphonious voice

Is escaping poisonous yet delicate lips.

Cerulean eyes, deeper than the ocean itself

Hiding my locus amoenus

Almost the antidote to my madness:

Lustrous Panacea.

Will you be there, scintillating,

When I am fully prepared to embrace it?

What I feel for you, something esoteric:

Not for everyone, I deduct.

Tête-à-tête, immersed in your mind,

Nothing more than just disparate souls

While you're driving me to the precipice of Insanity,

Corroding my compassionate heart

What a peaceful life I had:

"Halcyon" compared to now!

It would be vile, almost an Antithesis

To say you are not celestial...

Lustrous Panacea.

# Confessions

I wish I could find the words

to convey all those thoughts

and feelings for you, but

uncertainty and fears are

keeping them from breaking out

and fly away to freely dance

through these empty pages,

waiting for me to fill them

with your magical essence.

I don't want to sound banal,

dull, or even monotonous, but

when I come to these things, I

always end up sounding too

elaborate, falling in that

abyssal hole made of unsaid

whispers, awkwardly trying to

elucidate that concept that we

commonly call 'Love' for you

to fully grasp it, and make it

yours forever, carving it in

the depths of your soul.

Are you ready?

If only there were more words

to express the intricate way

you make me feel, I would make

use of them all, just for you;

but for today, just simple

words, nothing more, my

favourite remedy.

I love the way you

look at me with your

big bright eyes, while your

pure heart is messing with my

conscious, gently inviting my

intimate essence to dance with

you in an imaginary universe,

surrounded by a mystical

atmosphere.

I must confess

that I noticed the way you

crinkle your nose when you

laugh, or the way you play

with your soft hair, when you

get a little nervous: I

noticed, because that's one

of the many little things that

make you different from any

other person I have ever seen.

And I love it, so deeply.

Your eyes are like windows and

I believe I'm the only one who

can open them to your soul:

allow me to reach that idyllic

place we have so much

imagined when we were

younger, under a starry sky

and a scintillating moon, and

let me offer you my hand to take

you with me, and dive into

that infinite space.

Let me drown

in your calm, in the

serenity that makes me want to

hold your gaze, not run away.

Your eyes, the most precious

gem of my dreams: my treasure,

I vow to cherish you forever.

Your love, my only categorical

imperative: I'm aware it's a

risky game, but I'm gladly

willing to take the risk and

fight against thousand armies;

your happiness, your joy: my

best priorities. You know I

would run a thousand miles

barefoot, because I would

never miss your warm,

comforting smile.

I confess that I need you, like

a ship needs its captain:

you're essential to me, like

water to those wonderful red

roses in your garden. My knees

tremble, my body shivers, my

heart skips several beats: you

make me feel like a child in

front of that little game they

have always desired; boiling

blood in my veins is waiting

to explode: we, like fire and

gasoline in a plastic world,

shaking the Earth like the

strongest earthquake.

You turn

my world upside-down, just

with the slightest movement of

your cherry lips, while I'm

here, completely overwhelmed

 by this lethal force that

keeps pulling me down,

at your feet,

harmless.

# Fragile petal between hands of glass

My thin snow white arms

Lay on the cold floor,

While a fresh breeze

coming through the window,

procreate in me an odd sensation.

Numb to the feeling,

I observe the little lines

That pass through the

Numerous dots we

Commonly called "freckles".

My imperfect skin,

Full of blue little lines

That keep me alive,

Is reaching out to

The blinding light of the sun.

My shrinking body

Is slowly deteriorating,

Mixing with our common

Mother - the Earth - which

Takes back its creatures,

Once the time comes.

We reflect the light

And burn bright by ourselves,

Leaving nothing but a shadow

In the corner of our secret place,

Of our presumably safe house.

I sleep on the floor like a dog,

Swim free like a fish in the sea

And fly like an albatross through

The cloudy sky on our heads,

Leaving nothing but a

Feather for you to conserve.

I paint my issues on the canvas

Hung in the corridor of my life,

Using the brush I found under

A pillow, when my first tooth

Announced its departure.

I am fragile like a flower

During a cold winter night,

Falling down the tree of my

Self esteem, which withers

Morphing into the willow

of my never ending loneliness.

Dueling with my emotions,

I end up running away from them

And their overwhelming power.

Here I lay, like a fragile petal

between your hands of glass,

drowning in white acrylic paint.

I want to be free.

# Fairies among the stars

Walking hand in hand,

I feel the warmth of your heart

Beating to the rhythm of a melody,

The melody of our synchronized feet

While they stampede through the forest,

the one we've always dreamed of

That little oasis hidden among

our deepest and complex desires,

Because of our ineffable,

out of line way of living.

To you, I dedicate these words,

To the person who wipes my tears,

To the woman that makes me feel

Thousand of emotions that I have

Never imagined I could feel.

I sing these words for you to listen,

So you can finally acknowledge

My feelings: a tornado of chaotic thoughts

Dancing among the lines of my existence.

You are the muse of my rhymes:

To you I come, crawling through

The bushes of strawberries near

That little cottage that smells like home.

With you, I am free to recite my mind:

I swim among the deepness of your words

Unafraid, while your brown eyes finally

become the eighth wonder of the world.

Like a sunflower during the spring season,

I bloom and turn to you, my sun:

You're the source of my life,

The queen bee of my beehive.

Like a brave pirate,

I sail the seven seas

Incessantly searching for

The treasure that you are

The wave of our desires

Crashes against the chains

Of heteronormativity:

We're the exception to the rule.

Differently from any other creature,

We pirouette gracefully

On that thin stage made of ice,

Unaware of the danger of being us.

Floating around the lake,

And keeping up with

the cycle of the day,

We're fairies among the stars.

Like a package ready to deliver,

You teleport right to my door,

The door of a starry life

Encircled by Christmas lights.

You're the prohibited apple of

This big garden we call Earth.

Like atoms, we're so close to

Each other, but we don't dare to touch.

You're the masterpiece painted

In the canvas of my journey:

I pass a hand on the wet paint

Colouring your soul with magic.

Come to me, get closer

And let me play this harp

Whispering to the strings of

Your heart a soothing tune.

Connect your veins to mine

And give me the strength

To keep going, to live and thrive

In a world that wasn't made for us.

You're the precious pearl of my ocean,

Hidden inside a mollusc,

I find you sleeping like an angel

Lined up with the moon of my constellation.

# Dydreaming through the ashes of our downfall

Breathless illusions

Lethal burning lips,

Encircling the nest

With poisonous demands.

A freezing atmosphere,

Gently rubbing its dry fingers

Against delicate skin,

Catches the nucleus of our freedom.

We find ourselves

heading towards oblivion,

The land of uncertainty

broadening its horizons.

Suspense – melting bones,

Circling the town of ashes,

The town of make-believe

Where birds sing a dreadful song.

Crumbling thoughts, empty bodies

Laying down on the cold ground,

Waiting for the day the last drop dries off,

With no other choice but to turn and face this waterfall.

I, looking down from a high cloud,

Aim to be the worst I have ever been

Sipping vintage tree under the umbrella,

With a piece of cloth between lavender hands.

Run, run, run – there's no way out of this:

You are trapped inside this crystal ball,

Dancing among the goddesses of winter,

Playing a song performed by the orchestra of Death.

## Broken wings of a silent melody

I couldn't look at you any longer,

Your skin glowing like a meteor

Rusting my infinite tears

In the universe we float.

I didn't have it in myself:

All this time, all these years,

I've been having a lot of regrets,

Nothing but a crown of bones in my hands.

With the shiniest eyes,

Full of hope and joy,

Marble desires come to life.

You had to wish I was dead

before I could kill your aura.

Bury me underneath,

Down where the sun doesn't shine,

Where day and night are the same,

Where I can carve it in my mind forever.

Please, meet me anywhere but home.

I want you to stay away from me,

I want our souls to tip toe dance

Hush, don't say anything, honey

You're as fragile as a mirror

Spinning around the lonely room

The icy candles light up the atmosphere,

While we walk on the edge silently,

Afraid to break these empty promises.

Like a shadow I silently imitate you,

Day after day, rain after rain – then silence.

My words, worse than thousand arrows,

Pierce your solitary but golden heart.

Queen of hearts,

Sentence me to another galaxy

Demons I can't escape

Lately I just turn them into puppets

Permanent and eternal pain

Annihilating every inch of my essence.

Funny how innocence fleets

And vanishes under your naïve bridge,

I refuse to turn my head

I am afraid to know the truth

Thus I pretend I am as blind as a bat.

I promise that I see everything,

I see everything

And I tried everything

But everything isn't enough

Under your moon.

# Malibu

In the sun drinking fresh-squeezed lemonade,

you dance your way through the fireworks,

painting with your fingers the galaxy of my dreams.

Swimming through the vibrant blue waves,

A fresh feeling in my bones,

Brings me back on Earth, by your side

With hot sand under our feet,

While we stampede our way through life.

# Lunar dreams

I can still remember

When I was a pearl,

Mercury within my skin

Glowing in the dark,

Like the brightest source of light.

I came alive, when I was dreaming,

Dreaming about the moon landing,

While visiting factories of stars.

Scratching the wall, petrified,

I walk upside down towards you,

Until you pick me up again

And fix my pouring head.

# 31st of March

Like a silver line,

You encircle my soul

Giving it the strengh

to swing higher, and higher,

Til it reaches the clouds

That the red dragon fiercly protects.

In a huge field, full of daffodils,

You run with a crown of flowers

On your head - just us in the world.

Snowdon is not far away,

But your toes are stuck here, in the sand.

Your hands entangled to mine,

The million thoughts you have

Move through my nylon strands.

Your cerulean eyes hold the strengh of

A thousand waves, that crash

against my lavender skin.

Together, against the current,

We climb the imaginary wall

Between us, until our hands

wrap around each other's bodies.

# Memories

I've been seeing ghostly apparitions

Under the moonlight which, with

her veil, brings me a sense of comfort.

It penetrates the french window

enlightening the cold room,

While alone I stand,

with a box between the hands

counting the days

when your melody

was sweet and

not lethal.

# Absurd

With no direction,

no determination,

no strength, no skill,

my fingers keep typing

until there's nothing left,

but a signle inch of my

out of battery-creativity.

# Woods

Into the woods I walk:

trees surroundig me and my shadow,

walking hand in hand,

we get lost til we find each other

again and again.

# Dove

Oh white dove,

your bloody feathers

leaving your carcass by the border,

you suffer the thirst for power

that drives people crazy,

so you have limped ever since

a man decided he wants more than others.

# Guardian Angel

Warmer than fire

you keep me under your wing,

away from the gossip of mortals

and the mischievous games of the dead.

# Gender norms

*Hurry! Wash the dishes, prepare a meal!*

What am I to you

*Hurry! Clean the room, vacuum the floor!*

If not a vessel to fill up with your crude oil

*Go to work, buy a nice car!*

Holding it all together gets harder everday,

*Clean the room!*

Head between my hands, I sit on the floor

*Clear the table, have kids!*

Laying against the wall I punch it as hard as I can

*What about my grandkids?!*

Until bloody knocks find their way among my hairs

*Come on, make the bed!*

It's never been my full intention

*Take out the bin!*

To let you down.

*You always disappoint me.*

# To my younger self

Take one more step

and jump inside your mind,

into your memories

you'll swim.


Jump inside your heart,

into the thorns around it.

Grit your teeth, open your eyes

and fight till the sun comes out.


You'll find yourself.

# Hope

**Stronger**than a tornado

like a force of nature

a rainbow you'll ride.


You're sitting there,

just like a *dormant*volcano,

everything but inactive.


Lava flow will paint

your c o l o r l e s s  world.

# Love's slave

Love

It takes your breath away

and make you choke

alone, in a dark room.

# Poetry

Words.

Words.

Words.

I do not write words.


What I write is nothing but

   gnarled

         meaningless

              syllables

forced to stick


    together <>


inside a

      parallel                 cage.

# Survival

Remind me of the first time I had to pretend

- your arms entangled to mine, I run away

from you before losing my mind. Say something,

cuz silence is a killer and I'm its favourite prey.

# Childhood

I remember the days we used to play outside,

no thoughts or regrets, no hate or rivalry

just the fresh breeze of the countryside.

# Darkness

It was a cold, eerie night:

the moon was shining

even if partially obscured

by grey waving clouds,

as a howling wind was

adding to the city

an atmosphere of

suspense.

# Losing control

It was a fear induced by the unknown,

the fear of losing my mind, losing control.

I wasn't like that, I'm not like that

But today it was different.

Today it's another day.

And I was different.

# Rationality

My feelings were Rationality's favourite slaves,

and they weren't able to break free from this

suffocating pressure...they weren't strong enough

to finally win this cursed game. And so was I:

too weak to stop this never-ending struggle,

which was consuming every single inch of

my humanity.

# Thunderstorm

There was a raging thunder inside of me,

with a tornado of emotions, consuming

every part of my tormented soul.

I have thunder hidden inside,

and I can't let it out.

# Suffocating reality

Feeling gloomy and filled with misery,

I walk this path with my head underwater.

Is this the end?

# Opinions

Society brainwashed humans

to fear other's opinions of us:

we are constantly trying to make

people like us, and most of the

time we end up losing ourselves.

We almost become machines,

slaves of other people's approval,

we crave it, we want it, we need it.

more than oxygen itself.

# Failure - 404

Can you hear my voice?

**SOS**

Inaudible sounds leave my mouth

**SOS**

Am I even alive?

**SOS**

An emptiness takes over the house

**SOS**

Is this the end before the end?

**SOS**

I am left alone, forced to face a world,

**SOS**

Too silent and grey for us.

www.ingramcontent.com/pod-product-compliance
Lightning Source LLC
Chambersburg PA
CBHW021356160726
47994CB00007B/2982